BMS BOOKS
Oku Moe Moea
The dream which is bigger than I am

'It is ABOUT TIME that a story of this vision has arrived
to encourage children everywhere to believe in their talents
as the best contribution to our future.'
T. K Wikotu, Kaumatua

'The magic, I feel, is in the simplicity of your storytelling,
and the recognisability of your characters. Any adult who
has anything to do with the physical, spiritual, social and
emotional well-being of our nation's children, needs to
read this book.'
Glynis Knox, Assistant Principal, Frankton School, Hamilton,
New Zealand

'Oku Moe Moea - a book out of the ordinary, sharing the
tale of a child, his uniqueness and his talent, is almost
spiritual in tone. The links between generations, between
reality and faith, between friends...all carry us along
through the boy's growth and development. The reality of
his community is perfectly aligned with the reality of his
talent which isolates him from the mundane.'
Lynne R McAnulty-Street. Editor and reviewer for Booksellers NZ

The Principal and teachers of Frankton School,
Hamilton, New Zealand

6 November, 2014

Massey Street, Frankton, Hamilton 3204
Phone: 0-7-847 6726 • Facsimile: 0-7-847 7587
email: admin@franktonschool.ac.nz
www.franktonschool.ac.nz
Principal: Mrs Judy Dixon M.M, MMEN

To whom it may concern:

We give permission for Shona Hammond Boys to use any of our statements to support the publication of her book "Oku Moe Moea – The Dream Which is Bigger Than I Am".

Judy Dixon
Principal

Shakeeb Kalaam
Deputy Principal

Glynis Knox
Assistant Principal

Connor Chesham
Teacher

"Together we will develop a life long passion for learning & global citizenship"
"Ma te mahi tahi ka kawea e tatou nga whakaaronui oranga o nga akonga, ki nga iwi o te ao"

Oku Moe Moea

*The dream which is bigger
than I am*

SHONA HAMMOND BOYS

First Published in November 2014
Shona Hammond Boys
ISBN 978-0-473-29578-3

Published in January 2015 by BMS Books
An imprint of Business Media Services Ltd
5 High Street, Rotorua 3010, New Zealand
P.O. Box 6215, Whakarewarewa 3043, New Zealand
Tel: 64-7-349 4107; Mob: 027-209 6861
Email: ms@bms.co.nz
Web site: www.bms.co.nz

ISBN 978-0-473-30906-0
ISBN E-978-0-473-30907-7
ISBN Kindle 978-0-473-30908-4

Funds from this book support Children's Art Houses
www.arthouses.org.nz and www.icaf.org

DEDICATION

To the inspiring young creators in the Children's Art Clubs and Children's Art Houses in New Zealand whose open eyes brighten our future.

Creative Children Ensure Creative Communities.

ACKNOWLEDGMENTS

To the dedicated supporters who encourage creative children in the community to believe in their talents and dreams as our best force forward.

The illustrations on the blank pages at the end of some chapters are extracts from larger pictures donated by "Victory" for use to raise money for the New Zealand Children's Art Houses Foundation.

FOREWORD

Victory's story set in the eastern most part of New Zealand has the inspiration of a legend scanning space, place and set on a broad time scale.

It is about time that a story of this vision has arrived to encourage children everywhere to believe in their talents as the best contribution to our future.

As the Kaumatua (elder) of the New Zealand Children's Art House Foundation, I understand the struggle creative children have to develop individual artistic talents and hold on to their dreams, particularly if they are not supported by an understanding mentor.

T. K Wikotu

CHAPTER ONE

It was a veritable Eden, Victory's homeland. "Encased by beautiful rolling hills and bush-covered mountains, bisected by freshwater rivers and lapped by the blue waters of the mighty Pacific Ocean," the tourist guides said. He just thought it was his paradise in which to ride and to roam.

He was at one with it on his horse Storm when they rode the beach. The beach was his endless place, where he felt limitless, free and where every thought expanded for him.

He knew Storm felt the same. Together they made a handsome team. He rode as a dignified prince, without hesitation.

His father had taught him to ride when he was four. His mother used to ride but had stopped because of her troubles. She rode a bike now and never went far from home.

She had gained weight, but Dad still loved her. He kept a photo of her when she was younger. She asked him once why he still loved her. Was it for her beautiful body or because of her brains? Or was it because of her cooking? Dad had laughed, and said, "No. It's because I have a wonderful memory."

Victory loved his dad for that. As long as he could remember, mum was always having a baby or losing one. Nowadays neither parent talked about it, and Victory knew to keep quiet. He was their only, special child, the one who survived. He was their Victory.

Other relatives had big families and often tried to pass children on to his mum and dad, but neither of them wanted this, so they hardly went to family functions any longer.

Dad had his friends. They were a hardy outdoors lot, all big and strong. Victory worried that, because he was smaller, he would never grow up like them. His friends Legend and Righteous could, but he had little legs and was skinny compared to other boys in his class.

They nicknamed him Iti Waewae. Little Leg. He did not mind because he knew his classmates and what they were like; everyone had nicknames. It could have been worse.

He did not sing like other children. His home was very quiet and except for Little Fella and Parrie, his toy talking parrot, he had no toys. His mother used to sing well, everyone said, but he had never heard her except in his dreams. Victory had vivid dreams and recall.

He could remember in colour every detail of his mother bleeding when his last dead brother came. His father had been away in the bush, and Victory had just held his mother's hand in silence. She hardly made a sound. He thought she was amazing as she was very weak.

After the tiny baby had come, Victory carefully wrapped it in a cloth with the placenta and put them in a flax basket kete. He made his mother a cup of tea and got clean sheets for her before he ran down to a neighbour's for help.

In many ways, Victory was old before his time, like an ancient man in a small boy's body. "She's so heartbroken her bones are drying out," Victory heard the neighbours say.

"A merry spirit is good medicine." People tried to get her to laugh and invited her to things.

"She's not ready," Victory's dad said when they asked. Victory understood.

Victory's dad was a handsome, quiet man with long dreadlocks and a great smile, when it came. Three times Victory could remember him carefully holding the kete and leaving on his beautiful brown horse. Mum did not go with him. No one did.

The last time when his dad left, Victory's mum had held him tight and told him he would not have any brothers or sisters and that she had tried hard to have a sibling for him.

Victory's dad was either in the bush with his dogs hunting or with his mates. He did not go places with his wife because she was happy just to be home "for Victory". She knitted his clothes, washed them very clean and always had a meal ready at six o'clock. But she didn't talk to Victory much; her language was simple and short.

So Victory became much quieter than his peers and kept his thoughts to himself. He watched everything, intensely observing every detail, and he listened carefully to sounds. The clouds made music for him, and the bush, the beach and the river talked to him. "The birds know," he often said to comfort himself.

When he was eight, Victory was taken by his father into the bush on a long overnight ride. They slept out under the stars beside their horses.

The second day they stopped in a beautiful clearing and sat down. "These are your brothers and sisters," his father said, showing him five rimu trees and four totaras. "One day you will have your own tree." Victory realised these were the graves where the placentas and tiny bodies that had not come to life were buried. "These are your trees," Dad said as he named them all. Victory remembered the names of his five rimu sisters and four totara brothers.

Victory's dad Matua was a good bushman, well respected by other rangers. He loved being in the bush and mountains. He had no agenda about becoming rich.

Once, Victory rode with his dad and the men up into the majestic virgin mountain bush. There he felt the awesome presence of the ferns sleeping under tree groves. He breathed in the history of the ancient high forest canopy. He observed the monster tree ferns inhabiting the heart of the valleys. He saw the spectacular tall giants which pierced the skyline. He heard and watched the birds. He bathed in crystal streams.

And so he understood the relaxed contentment of the men as they rested after billy tea and tucker, while their horses grazed in a clearing. The clearing was created when a great tree had fallen, and there was a hole in the sky.

CHAPTER TWO

Victory was Vedic in nature. He could not hurt a living thing. He adored the bush, the beach and the river. But he was not so sure about other people.

It was to art that Victory went for comfort and excitement. He could draw for hours, never noticing the time. He became very observant and tried to draw many things by direct surveillance.

By three years of age, he was quite obviously an artist. He had begun scratching patterns in the sand almost as soon as he could walk. He often preferred collecting shells and arranging them in patterns to swimming. He constructed driftwood houses on the beach. His houses lasted longer than other children's because his were sturdy.

Sometimes Victory made insects or birds. Whereas other children made small things, he could build very large accurate kowhaiwhai patterns, repeating them accurately in refined detail. Everything Victory did was fresh and carefully produced, well thought out first.

Teachers at his first school found him curious. His handwriting was beautiful, and he quickly learned to read. The teachers thought his mother had taught him, but she just asked him to read to her each day when the little books came home.

She could not read, and she hoped that Victory could help her to learn. He realised this and never said a word, just reading very slowly and carefully pointing to everything as if he was learning it himself.

But Victory could read a newspaper. No one knew this. He kept it to himself. He did not want to be different, because different was difficult. It was hard for him to "play" with other children, because they snatched and grabbed things. So he quickly learned that their games were silly and teasing.

Everyone took his drawings, even his teacher, so he was careful with his sketchbook. He sat quietly at school; he spoke carefully and did not say anything to anyone unless asked, and then he was most polite and cautious.

He did not go to other children's homes after school. His mother did not like that. He guessed it was because then he would have to invite them back, and she did not want visitors. It was a good enough childhood because he knew his parents loved him and that many children were not so lucky.

Victory's parents were also older than other children's in his class, and they were poor. They rented their back house, and because his mother did not work, Dad provided from his trappings, fishing and hunting. The family did not own a phone or a car. For all special events, they put down a hangi and Dad's friends came.

Mum's relatives lived miles away, and so did her

friends. Because her reading and writing were poor, she had little contact with them unless they arrived to stay. Then they slept on the floor in Victory's bedroom and snored.

People thought it strange that Victory's mother did not want to go out and work. Sometimes social workers came. They always held her hand. She took no medicine and would not go to the doctors. She was very careful about herself. "Look after your mother," Dad would always say when he went off. Sometimes he added, "She is precious."

Victory always thought his mum would die soon. So he usually hurried home to make sure she was still there. She had beautiful long black hair and lovely eyes. When he got home from school, she always said, "Welcome my son." He knew she adored him.

It was too far to go to the library, and it cost to take out books from the library. They did not get a newspaper or have TV. Victory's mother wore glasses, ever since an accident when she was little. Victory thought this was why she found reading very hard, but he also wondered whether she had worn her eyes out with her tears. People called her the rainmaker. Her parents had died when she was little, and she had been in many foster homes.

At night, she watched the stars and she told Victory, "We admire the stars too fondly to fear the darkness." The celestial heavens and the cosmos seemed to talk to her and keep her calm.

Neither Mum nor Dad mentioned God or gods. They did not need to, for they worshipped and respected life itself so much.

Dad often brought Mum wildflowers when he returned from his journey. She knew the place where he got them because they had gone there when they were young, in their first summers together. She did not grow flowers, but she walked slowly past the florist shop downtown when she went out briefly for the supplies.

Victory was fascinated with flowers. The colours, scents, shapes and softness thrilled him. He did not think anyone knew about this aspect of his personality and he tried hard not to show it. Boys and flowers were not supposed to go together - it should be a girl thing.

CHAPTER THREE

The girl Victory liked lived next door. He liked her energy and her smile. She waved to him but never spoke. He knew her name. Maria. Maria was always singing as she went past his house. She had lots of friends and a cat and a dog with whom she was very gentle.

She was wonderful to watch through the bedroom window when she jumped on the trampoline. Victory had not been on a trampoline in his life, and he thought that the things she did were very risky. She always came up laughing even when she fell hard.

She had a lot of older brothers and sisters because two families had merged. She was the baby of the new partnership.

Victory did not tell Legend about his fondness for Maria as he could tell Legend liked her too.

Legend lived in the next door street and he was Victory's best friend. They had been friends since they first met at baby school.

Legend had all the confidence in the world. He

rode bareback triumphantly as a conquering hero. He was loud, jolly, strong and going to be an All Black. Everyone believed that. His mother said she had seen him in a dream when she was six years old. She had known she was going to have a strong child called Legend.

He had other brothers and sisters. Righteous, his little brother always rode on the back of Legend's horse, but soon he could be riding on his own. He was nearly Legend's size already.

Righteous got his name from his Uncle Righteous, whom he looked a lot like. Victory often wondered whether he was Uncle Righteous' child, because around here you never really knew who was whose.

Righteous never got in the way of the two boys' friendship, because he was his own man.

Legend had helped Victory's mum by cleaning the spouting and the drains after the flood when Matua was away in the bush. He could fix anything and lift twice the weight that Victory could. Legend just laughed. He had great respect for "Me old matey Vic". He saw wisdom in his friend others did not yet know about, and he knew that Victory was 100 per cent loyal as a mate. "Vic, me old matey," he would say, "tell me what you think." Legend was always astonished at what Victory would tell him and wondered where all this knowledge came from.

Legend never did any homework and did not bother with anything but sport at school. He too seemed older than his years and, in his own way, was an indomitable leader. Victory thought Legend could rule the world if he wanted.

They were an odd pair, and people noticed how busy they were compared to other children. But everyone smiled at them as they rode the trails around the neighbourhood. They had an air of freedom about them and were already local identities at eight years old. No one worried that they were riding big horses without parental supervision or crash helmets because the boys were so capable. They rode bareback, usually without shoes and carried very little besides small backpacks. They rode in all weathers and seldom had coats or hats.

Legend's household had one person coming in the front door as another went out the back door. Half the people did not seem to know each other, although they always greeted the others like family and threw down some food to share. People slept in every room and there were mattresses on the floors, even in the corridors.

The house always looked like an earthquake had hit it. The big TV screen blasted out rugby and horror movies. It went day and night. The music and conversations were loud. Everyone drank beer and left cans on the floor, and most visitors smoked. Legend's mum did not seem to mind everything being in chaos around her. There was no order anywhere.

Victory did not go to that house, but met Legend after school at the gates and made arrangements to swim, fish and ride with him. They went somewhere outdoors two nights a week.

CHAPTER FOUR

Both boys had an interest in the Children's Art House club. It fascinated them for different reasons.

For Victory, it was the highlight of his week to go to club sessions and look at the books on the Children's Art House shelves. This was his library. He memorised the pictures he saw there and recalled them at night in his bed.

He loved the gallery filled with children's art and the ceilings draped in banners and panels. He loved the masks, the makings, the weaving, the mosaics, the models, the landscapes, the murals, the sculptures and just everything made and planned there.

He loved the two Children's Art House rules of Love Art and Be Kind. Victory knew that small acts of kindness add up to mountains of goodness.

And he knew creativity was very important to human beings. He knew that for him, it was not a luxury; it was a necessity. He always felt better after he had had time in the studio, painting, making or drawing out his ideas. He was always so busy he did not usually notice what others were doing, but they all noticed him and wished they could be like him.

He also knew his father begrudged the weekly gold coin fee for each club session. Dad thought he should be getting fitter by joining a gym. Victory really appreciated his mother for sticking up for him to stay in the club.

Legend, on the other hand, just loved having a go at anything and did not care how it turned out and did not think much about it. He was a social creature and loved talking to everyone. Other club members thought he was a star. Art club sessions just filled time for him when there was no rugby training. He sat next to Victory and loved watching what Victory did and tried to copy.

But no one could copy Victory, even if he tried to show them how. His lines were sure and clear, and in a few lines he could describe so much. He could make things seem far away, and others seem close up. He could illustrate myths and history and put people in his drawings, many people, doing all sorts of activities. He could draw his club mates accurately, and they all wanted him to do them a portrait. He never had any formal lessons and the Art House coordinator just left him alone. "He is happy here, and that's all that matters," the teacher said as he sharpened the pencils and put out the paint.

The truth was that the Art House coordinator did not know what to do about Victory, and he had never seen a child artist like him before. He just hoped Victory would find his own way in life, but he did not have a clue as to how to help him. None of his friends knew either, not even the senior artists in the town. They did not believe the drawings the tutor took to show them. "Holy cow," the eldest artist said on sighting a piece by Victory. "He will put us all out of a job."

And so it was that people knew about Victory's drawings. They were always trying to get one from him, but they did not offer help. This only made him quieter. He drew on anything he could lay his hands on. He drew on his hands when he had no paper, and he knew to wash them off before his father saw.

CHAPTER FIVE

In the skate park, Legend was a star and Victory just sat watching him. It gave him much pleasure watching the flips and impossibilities Legend managed like bouncing a ball while skating at speed. Victory knew not to try and copy Legend doing anything physical. Just as Legend knew not to try and copy Victory doing anything creative or artistic.

For a few months, Victory used to sit and draw Legend while he jumped and twisted around high above his board. But the bigger boys came and took Victory's drawings and put pressure on him to draw more. He began to avoid the skate park.

The skate park was ugly, anyway. The drawings, signatures, and words on the walls were scribble and offensive to him. He could visualise a most exciting colourful mural on the skate park walls, with figures leaping in excitement and with an energetic glory. He knew he had the ability to do that work now if he had the tools and materials. He sensed the boys who put graffiti on the walls were aware of his ability and were jealous; this made him uncomfortable around them.

They had formed a gang and met there to make trouble. They were idle roamers and spoke rudely to passersby and frequently swore about people. They kicked their dogs and hit their horses.

It was not so much their bad language that offended him but the way they treated each other. Blame, pain, shame and put-downs were tossed out to each other in a culture Victory thought stunk. He wanted no part in it, but Legend could ride over the top of it and cope.

Victory decided he would have to give up going to the skate park with Legend, and it made him sad. "It's okay, me old matey," said Legend when Victory told him. "You've got better things to do." Victory loved him for understanding.

On the beach, Legend and Victory constructed remarkable driftwood houses. People often slept in them in the heat of the summer.

Legend dragged big pieces of trunks and put them where Victory said. Victory had an overview of the finished house. Each house had a quirk to it and was fascinating to those passing by who stopped and took pictures. From nothing, it seemed Victory could visualise something beautiful and functional. He could assess the materials lying on the beach and build with them. The beach houses were strong and durable and usually lasted all through the coming winter.

He could build bush houses too. No one had taught him how. He had just worked it out.

Around these totally recycled houses, Victory used a stick to scratch beautiful patterns in the sand or soil. These patterns were not sandcastles but original masterpieces. They were his flower paintings, his kowhaiwhai and his garden.

He knew that the tide would get them, but he loved the scale and transient nature of his patterns. They reminded him of a favourite song he often heard Maria singing: "One day comes. One day goes. Here today. Gone tomorrow. Someone laughs. Someone cries. Time it comes. It comes to fly."

CHAPTER SIX

Because Victory was a frail child, he caught every cold and infection. He had been well premature and hard to raise this far. Not like Legend, who had never had a cold and did not know what it was to feel ill.

When he had his days in bed, Victory went deep under the blankets and invented far-away places in his mind. There he built amazing cities with the latest technologies. Like sonar, solar and everything wireless built from nanotechnology. People had flying cars and there were no schools, as people had small computers connected to them. In these cities, the computers were brighter than people and told them what to do.

It all fell into place for him under those warm blankets with his hot-water bottle. It occupied his mind for hours, thinking what the future would be like. But always as he fell asleep, it was the big trees and the beach that meant the most to him. He could feel himself floating out with the tide and going down with the sun.

In his sleep, he flew and visited distant planets and cosmic systems. He loved their colours, their swirls and structures. Sometimes it was hard waking up to his barren bedroom in his far flung land. He had never discussed his night dreams with anyone because Victory had no mentor. And he was uncertain and fearful, doubting his normality more and more as he grew to see that he was not like others around him.

He sensed that he might have chosen to come here and have this life experience. He knew he was lucky to be here; that it had been a big struggle to be born. He felt vulnerable whenever he thought of his brothers and sisters and whenever his mother said, "Take great care Victory," as he went off without her to school.

He regarded it as a great privilege to be here and periodically felt guilty about his flying away dreams. He did not want to worry his mother about them as she had dreams of her own.

Dad called them both his dreamers. He was a practical man and had no time for make-believe or fantasies. "You have got to get on with it and cannot spend your time sitting around dreaming," he would say to Victory. As time went by, Victory knew to keep very quiet about the thoughts in his head. He knew not to mention his wild imaginings or show his drawings. But he was concerned at the distance growing between him and his father.

Victory came to the Art House for comfort and to strengthen his soul. He came to find out who or what he was, and what he could be. He was a vision seeker, wanting to have light.

He operated almost entirely as a visual idealist, with vivid mystical and supernatural mental pictures flooding his mind. He saw things of extraordinary beauty and complexity and things that others were incapable of imagining.

He had significant foresight and was able to see things that had not yet come into being. At the river, he could work out how to build a bridge across it. At the beach, he could see groins stretching out to sea and imagine a big port. In the bush, he visualised ways of protecting the valleys and streams, the birds and the natural environment from the dangers of mankind.

While he drew his wonderful patterns, he pondered on these things. After a session of drawing, he was tired, although not because of the drawing, but due to the ideas that flooded his mind.

He was as tired after a three hour drawing stint as Legend was after strenuous football training. His mother seemed to understand and ran him a hot bath with precious lavender oil in it. His mother believed lavender oil healed many things and was relaxing. The bath was a luxury thing in their household. It was allowed only once a week. Every other time there was only a quick shower, as power bills were hard to keep down. The family had a one-bar heater, and just put on extra layers of clothes in the winter instead of lighting a fire.

Lavender was his mother's perfume. She put it in every drawer to stop insects. She put it on his pillow to help him sleep, and she put it on his handkerchiefs to help his breathing. She used it for stings and itches and shampooed his hair with it to try and stop nits. But nits were epidemic in his school, and both Legend and Righteous got them and passed them on to Victory.

The school nurse called them one-by-one to her office one Tuesday. They had to sit with a horrid special cap on out on benches where everyone could see them and wait 20 minutes for the smelly treatment to work. It was humiliating.

Victory struggled with the idea of killing the little creatures in his hair, but everyone else just wanted them gone. He had viewed them at home with his mother's magnifying glass and watched what they did. They fascinated him. He knew the eggs would hatch soon and watched them carefully. His mother, of course, doubly cleaned his sheets and pillows and clothes and vacuumed the floors madly, over-tiring herself with activity after the notice came home.

It was normal to get nits, school sores, runny noses and colds in the dark lands. The area of town where he lived was on the outskirts and known as the dark lands, because the lighting was poor and the footpaths cracked. The curbing and channelling was scarce, and the houses all had trouble with flooding.

There were troubles inside the houses because of unemployment, crime and toxic relationships. Poor housing and overcrowding stretched everybody's nerves. Some people said it was not fair that Victory's family had a house to themselves, even if it was tiny. But Mum's social worker friend had sympathy for Mum because they had been best friends at school, and so she looked out to make sure things were as good as possible for them all.

Everyone knew everyone, and everything was observed and reported back on the town's grapevine. As Victory grew up, he quickly learned to come in and close the gate and say very little to anyone. Anyway, he had to close the gates because of the roaming dogs. Mostly they were pig hunting dogs and not registered and not to be trusted.

Dad kept his dogs well under control and away from the town. They were highly trained and healthy. So were the horses. They were never beaten, and they loved Matua and would do everything he asked, but he cautioned Victory, "You cannot teach a dog algebra."

CHAPTER SEVEN

Dad's father had been a bush man too. He died in an accident crossing a swollen river. Dad had to criss-cross that river 28 times to get to his father's old house. He was not going there so often now and the house was slowly decaying.

Dad's mother had died in child birth, along with her last baby. The rest of the children were farmed out to relatives, but Matua had stayed on up the valley.

Victory never even knew his grandparents. Not like some of the children in his school, who were being raised by their grandmothers and grandfathers, if they were still alive.

Victory noticed how few kids had fathers, and he wondered about it. People said the fathers had gone to the city to work. He was not sure about that. Some had gone to the mines in Australia where the money was supposed to be good. Some were in prison for growing weed.

People said Dad had stayed and looked after his

father because they were almost identical. He took the loss of his father hard, and he scarcely knew his brothers and sisters or where they were today.

Victory knew his father did not like the town and was only there because of his mother. She needed to be near a hospital.

Victory also knew that his father feared for his son's future. He saw doors slamming in Victory's face if Victory could not learn to conform. He saw disappointments and failure for his son if he strove to become an artist. But for Victory there was never any choice or hesitation; he had come into the world to express himself through being creative. He felt that one day he would have to leave his father, but he could not imagine leaving his mother. He was uncomfortable about being silent with his dad.

Granddad had had a friend who was once an artist and it was said he was still living around here somewhere. People called him "The Elder." Victory thought he had seen him out walking several times while he sat sketching at the river-bank. The Elder had been a big man, a bush man and a good rider.

Apparently in his older years he had led the movement to save the big trees from milling. He did not have a name. He did not have a legal birth certificate and did not know how old he was.

The Elder had grown up in a handmade bush hut built into the side of the hill. Victory knew that these huts were very warm because of the way they were woven together and constructed. No one was allowed to live in them now. Most of them were burnt down by the council years ago as not suitable for human living.

To Victory's mind, the modern houses were puny

in comparison. Victory was very interested in making environmental constructions which did no damage and which could, after a time, be recycled back into the environment. He planned to build his own, unique house one day.

He studied the homes of all the insects and animals, and he loved bird nests. He saw how birds built their nests in river banks and logs. He watched them working hard to collect the materials and stockpile food.

Very little escaped Victory's beady eyes. He could sit very still for hours and watch the family life and the wars between insects. He learned about survival, about weapons like stabbers and suckers, tongues and stings.

At times, he would have insects crawling all over him as he drew, even bees. They did not sting him. He loved bees and worms. The social behaviour of ants fascinated him, and the life of the colonies of ants and bees gave him much food for thought. None of this he shared with anyone else, even Legend.

Legend was too busy just being alive with joy. At the river, Legend thrashed around in the water, dive-bombed and loved swimming underwater. He loved water play.

Victory would just sit and watch the water flow and think about the current and the swirls and the way the tide changed the river or the volume after rain. He loved seeing Legend so happy in his world.

Legend lived in the moment, but Victory lived in the future and quickly had accumulated significant understandings of the past. He believed that no one could progress the future by obliterating the past. He believed that the individual and society should be invested in equally. He saw the world as one planet and people as one people, living on a globe in crisis. He looked for the balance and harmony in situations at every level.

All this was natural to Victory. He knew no different. He saw that a world of superficial brilliance, of appearances only, conflicted with everything he knew. He wanted nothing false.

After his last premature sibling had been laid to rest, he had made a hand puppet. Victory named him. Little Fella. Little Fella was his conversation companion about matters of the soul. Victory would lie in bed and quietly tell Little Fella everything that had happened to him or that bothered him. Sometimes he would take Little Fella to school in his backpack, especially if he were going sketching after school.

Mum and Dad knew how much he loved his little man. Dad thought he should be growing out of this toy by now, but Mum cautioned Dad to let the boy be.

Victory always spoke quietly to Little Fella so that no one else could hear. Little Fella was the only being in the world who knew all about Victory. Legend knew about Little Fella and he understood how much Victory talked to his creation in the wee dark hours of the night.

Legend had brothers and sisters and a house full of people to talk to. Victory had Little Fella.

Little Fella was a *papier mâché* hand-held puppet with a tapestry hand glove. The index finger went into the neck, and the little finger and the thumb went into the sleeves and became the hands. The puppet's head was the size of a tennis ball, and his hair had been very neatly laid out in the only wool colours available to Victory, who had cut them into small equal parts. Then he had searched the baby-school scrap box and was thrilled to find that his favourite material was just big enough for sewing up a glove. He hand-sewed the dress carefully together and carefully mixed a little paint up for the face colour. He did not have much time and thought he could have done better.

But classes were always like this. Things had to be put away before story time and home time. One teacher observed him closely and testified to the group that, yes, a child had made that puppet in 30 minutes. No one believed her. Victory was very lucky to get Little Fella into his bag and take him home because that teacher wanted to keep him as a record of her good teaching ability. This incident was Victory's first realisation that what he made was desirable to others.

Victory's speech was delayed. He hardly spoke at all before he went to school. Victory really only began talking to Little Fella. When his mother heard him talking in sentences to his puppet, she had wondered how he learned to talk so easily. She did not tell anyone, because being an only child she knew others would think she was showing off.

Victory had gone from no speech to using big words very quickly. But he did not use big words freely to others, only to Little Fella.

His mother wondered where these words originated. Where did he hear such big words? Some she did not even know the meaning of. She did not realise he was reading everything he ever saw, printing on signs, in shops and pieces of literature delivered into the mailbox. Nor did she realise that Victory remembered what he read.

And he loved numbers too. Maths came just as easily as reading. He had quickly realised by himself that it was cheaper to buy in bulk.

At school, he did not write anything unless asked, and then he made sure that it was like the other children's work. He only wrote three lines of a story, if that was what the teacher held up as a model.

He took all his cues from what was on the board every day. "The 'Ank' family today," she said. Thank, bank, sank. In seconds, Victory thought clank, blank, drank, stank, crank, Frank, prank, blank, yank, and rank. But he did not say anything or write them down. He had a growing awareness that no one knew what was in his head or the head of another person, and that everyone was a mystery to each other.

To occupy his mind, he gave himself mathematical problems to solve. And he had a voracious appetite for rich vocabulary, noticing all the fine degrees of subtlety in people's expressions. He was highly stimulated by other languages and different types of people or unusual and diverse situations.

Victory had a global mind. Even though he lived in this beautiful, remote place, he had seen the map of the world and had a fair idea of the size of the planet and the distances between countries. He had found out the distance to the moon and sun. He had exceptional curiosity about the stars and other planets. Whereas Mum looked at them and thought how lovely they were, he was trying to assess the distance to them and where they lay in relation to the sky's patterns.

Stars were his friends, and often at night he would look out his window and gaze at them with a head full of questions. How heavy were they? How did they stay in orbit? He knew the sky could not fall on you – it's only air. But he realised there were huge flying objects in space that must be bigger than earth and that they could collide and blow up at any moment.

His intellectual curiosity and intuitive powers bothered him. He could not see anyone around him who remotely resembled him in any way. Sometimes he thought he must be an alien of sorts.

Without knowing it, Victory had already formed a deep philosophy about life. Racism and violence had no part in his life code. He adopted the least aggressive pathway in everything.

He believed knowledge gained based on life's experiences, and he told Legend, "You have to turn over a lot of stones to find a princess under one." Often, what he said puzzled Legend.

Victory became acutely interested in lyrical beauty, in rhythms and repeating sounds. He loved harmonious creativity and tranquil solutions. He loved the sounds of a working beehive.

He wondered deeply. Did enlightened men exist along with Neanderthals? And he worked out that religion was just an interpretation of what you discover or what you believed or did not believe was God or soul.

He wanted his personal best, nothing less. He did not believe there had been a perfect person but thought that we were all individually responsible for our mana.

He felt that prehistoric peoples could have had no beginnings; they may have always existed throughout time. He envisioned a prehistoric and a new technologically advanced race that could transcend physical planes of space and time. He saw worlds within worlds, within worlds, in macro- and micro- form. And, as he pondered such things, he walked along his street to school with his hands behind his backpack, comforted because Little Fella was in it.

The other boys noticed him and often talked about him. "He's strange," they said. "He does not fit in with us around here."

"He is always drawing and doesn't want to play with us. He is very good at art," one said.

"Yeah, so what?" another challenged.

They fought about him amongst themselves and argued whether they should leave him alone or shake him up.

They did not talk about him when Legend was with them because Legend was king around here, and Victory was Legend's friend. It was a friendship none of them understood. They respected Legend because he fought back, and because one punch from him hurt.

They all knew Victory would not fight back or answer back to their teasing. In fact, they did not know anything about him at all, except that his dad Matua was well-respected, and they did not want to get in trouble with him.

CHAPTER EIGHT

And so it was one fine afternoon when Victory sat drawing on the river bank and The Elder noticed him. "That's Matua's boy," he thought to himself from the stopbank. Victory was too engrossed to notice, but even with his old eyes and from a distance, The Elder could see that Victory's work was substantial. "I must keep track of him," thought The Elder.

It had been a long time since his old friend, Victory's grandfather, had died. Fondly, The Elder remembered their long-ago friendship and the way he had been encouraged by that one person when he lived far up the valley. Now here was his friend's grandchild, an only boy, sitting alone drawing at the river bank.

The Elder's heart softened. Although he came from a very large family, the only other person who had encouraged him as an artist was his grandmother. And an artist he was. For part of his early life, he was able to indulge in his dreams and talents, but the depression and the war had wiped out all his dreams and left him shaky on his legs from an injury. His sketchbook had been stolen and not returned. He lost heart and at the time had not been able to afford another book.

Like others around, he became a bushman and worked for the mill. He showed the company where the big trees were and he got money for each telling. Now he deeply regretted having done this, and was guardian of the last patch of pristine native forest where sacred trees had been kept fenced off and protected. He wanted all the land to go back to nature, and the ocean and rivers to be protected from corporate exploitation.

The Elder had been called 'The Elder' for many years. No one knew how old he was. In those days, registration of babies was not law. Families would not leave the bush to go and fill in papers which they could not read. Many people could not write well and had no signature. They did not particularly want one, nor to join the increasingly imposing British settlements which were interfering with their lifestyle. They were just whanau, family. Tangata whenua, people of the land. In The Elder's community, everyone was mother or father to all the children. Young children often minded babies. Extended family members fed children and everyone belonged to each other.

The Elder had a vast knowledge of the plants and trees and the times for planting, and the tides, sun, moon and stars. He knew his language well and had a highly developed memory of the oral history passed down to him about his ancestors.

When he was about ten, he had to go to school, which meant crossing the river many times on his horse. If he was late, he got caned by the stern missionary master, and if he spoke his own language, he also got caned. He was to learn a new language and become civilised.

He did not stay at school long, and he remembered his grandmother's teachings. He had seen his first fairy person when he started school. Some called white people the ghost people, others called them fairy people or pakeha.

The Elder felt the weight of these different people's arrival upon his community. Change was being thrust upon his family rapidly, and it was permanent. His peers all wanted guns, to go to town and to drive a car.

He just wanted to run into the bush and hide, draw, ride his horse along the river beds and fish. He loved art. Especially if it reflected his homeland and the wonderful stories his elders told him. He could draw accurate portraits. He admired the fine weaving and beautiful carving prepared for the five meeting houses representing his tribe.

His fine ear helped him learn to speak English well before other family members and even without much schooling he learned to write it.

He cleaned windows for money. Later in life he went into and out of National Parliament, presenting submissions on land rights, ownership, environmental matters and legalities. He was a formidable advocate for justice and truth. He studied law and became cultural representative for various groups concerning his area.

But he had no children of his own and had fostered many, supported by his wife. They ran a receiving home, and anyone in trouble could turn up there day or night and would be given a bed and shelter. He was seldom without a baby in his home and small children running around, as he was particularly compassionate towards abandoned mothers.

For a while, after the war, he exercised revenge violence and fell into bad ways, but he regretted it. He was a pacifist nowdays and hated violence of any kind.

The war had not been kind to his whanau. They had lost many young men. Those who came back were touched with grief and many had damaged minds. Many young women had married outside his culture.

The modern world brought with it serious temptations, like speeding in cars, drink, drugs and gambling. He had watched the massive changes occurring amongst his people as if it were a bad, sad play. His people now seemed like just relics and remnants of what had been so beautiful and dear to him.

Often, he sat and studied the young children, his beautiful mokopuna. They were handsome and physically strong. He longed to stop the tides of change sweeping across his country, even though he knew it was irreversible. He was nearing the end of his life; a life he knew could not be replicated in future.

He feared for the young ones and wept. He wept because of what he knew was the difference for those living in today's world from living in his childhood world. He was acquainted with grief, tangi and death, and he did not fear his death. But he feared what would happen to the children who had to live in the world they were inheriting.

He apologised to them for the state of the world around them. They had so little chance of knowing who or what they were, or developing individual personalities or being-ship. He saw little chance for them growing up at one with existence, and being able to be alone with nature, freely, in a relaxed bliss.

And so The Elder was thrilled to see this boy who was different sitting by himself sketching on the river bank. He was cheered to realise that this was the descendant of his long lost buddy, and he pledged to become friends with Victory.

He told his wife that night that he was going to support another child from a distance and she just said sweetly, "What's new?" He added, "He goes to the Children's Art House."

Sometimes, she despaired of her mate when he disappeared into the bush going walkabout or was off on a horse somewhere. It was hard not to be concerned now age had left him frail. He had no teeth and his stomach played up.

And she was concerned about so many others. Being a big man's wife is not easy, because all the problems come to the door. The relatives always used their place to camp over when they came to town. Mostly they did not tell her when they were coming, and she was expected to feed multitudes at a moment's notice.

She was expected to keep quiet in meetings. However, she had strong points of view, and there had been some nasty family events where she had been hurt.

He was fearful to leave her alone now. They had been together a long while. No one knew how long or when and if they were married, because there were no papers or photographs.

He had claims to land and so did she, and these were still in tribunals with the government. They lived in an old Justice Department house which was part of some claim that had not been settled, so they lived every day with uncertainty.

Her days were spent with family members and visitors. Nobody knew how many people lived there, because at any time the numbers varied. Some people stayed weeks, while others stayed days or overnight. The authorities got tired of trying to track people down. Social workers did not like to visit, and the Government did not know what to do about benefits. She got tired of making cups of tea for the next counsellor or agency worker who called in to fill out papers or make their recommendations. After all, she was the one who was doing the work, day and night.

Her mood changed from delight to anger very quickly as she listened to the stories of the families in need who arrived on her doorstep. She had camped out with her mate in protest about land matters. She had lived in tents through cold winters and gone to countless protest marches and meetings. She felt strongly about the inconsistencies over land ownership.

Apart from significant knowledge of her culture, music and language, she was fluent in English. She grew up in the most eastern point of her country and had been educated in a bilingual school, and there exposed to the Christian church culture. Part of her upbringing was to know about the forest plants and their healing properties, and she enjoyed this knowledge and loved sharing it with the young mothers who were sheltering in her home. Her father was an engineer and scholar and taught her the finer points of life. Most of all, he taught her to think for herself. So she became an independent and strong-minded woman.

One of her major concerns was that today, mothers could not deliver their babies. Her mother and grandmother had delivered their babies deep in the bush, had breastfed their babies and stayed well and healthy. But today's babies had many ailments, and the mothers had many issues. They were not always supported by the fathers and their babies often got chest and ear infections. Many young mothers just wanted to party and go out and behave randomly.

The Elder's wife was always talking about the need for routine and hygiene. But things so quickly spiralled into chaos around these young parents. She thought that jobs and money would help but, more than that, values needed to be changed. She kept talking about old ways, which did not go down well with some of the young people around her. "She talks in the past," they said and disregarded her.

Her health was ailing, and she felt she was losing ground from the centre out. She knew that one dies from the centre outwards. She tried to get time to reflect and meditate in order to restore her tired self, but in a home like theirs it was impossible to find individual space.

The Elder and his wife had moved from the bush into the outskirts of town so that they would be nearer the small local hospital. Neither of them particularly wanted to make such a move, but they thought it was best to be sensible. They had seen many old people die up the valleys, and some could have lived much longer with better help.

The town and its ways were quite foreign to them. They got a benefit and came down through the main street to receive it on Thursdays. Benefit day. There they had a meat pie and cup of tea treat for lunch and met other friends in The Bake House.

But benefit day was also court day, and it was hard to watch so many young ones going to court for petty crimes. Most were about fines unpaid, but increasingly they noticed more and more stealing and violence amongst their youth. Their people seemed unsettled.

They disliked seeing all the tourists taking photos of their people. The tourists were usually European, blonde, with blue eyes. They appeared to be educated travelling students or wealthy people on an overseas experience.

Some came from the big smoke, and they may just as well have been from another land. Like the young girl social workers who came to visit their home. These were of European stock who lived on the wealthy side of the big city and who got a degree and were then given a job to come down here and sort out local people. It did not work. Worlds were in collision here.

You were not accepted here unless you had lived here about a quarter of a century. When everyone knew your name and you had been tried and tested, then you were without suspicion.

But the pace of change was rapidly kicking into the district and nothing was certain now. Each night The Elder and his wife went for a slow walk along the river bank. He said his chants and she joined him in the blessings. They were not going far these days.

Both had walking sticks, beautiful carved sticks from their ancestors. They wished the young people had a reconnection with their culture.

Sometimes they thought that teenagers were aliens, like unexploded time bombs, yet they treated everyone as salvageable. They thought their young people had the trapped-animal-syndrome and that youth had lost their connection with nature.

The Elder and his wife could remember the preciousness of living with animals. The joy of eeling, milking a cow by hand, walking miles in the rain and not worrying about getting wet, were clear memories. They were shocked that young people would not drink milk straight from a cow and had to get it packaged from a shop. They could remember noticing the small changes in nature around them as the seasons changed. They knew the real meaning of whanau was relationships, not blood.

The local council servicing the area often called on The Elder to perform ceremonies to show the equal recognition of the races. At opening or closing events he would be asked to say a blessing, or he would be asked to show distinguished guests around the meeting houses. This would mean providing food and sometimes accommodation, ceremonial song and speeches which often required historical explanations.

In his heart The Elder despaired, and had no time for the council. It was largely comprised of white, wealthy farming stock, or modern-day orchardists who paid his people sometimes below minimum wage to work on their properties picking and packing fruit. Many farmers had become very rich from farms on land confiscated in his grandfather's time, and he found no integrity or empathy with them and their rich talk.

What they called 'farming,' he saw as the rape of the land and thought that blatantly dishonest and destructive decisions had been made against his elders. Nonetheless, he cautioned his young people to cooperate and rise above the issues they faced with dignity and pride.

The school truancy issues bothered him. He saw them at the heart of the crime and first offending of the young. He did his best to be optimistic, to encourage education and show empathy to all, to be gentle but firm and to praise good efforts.

CHAPTER NINE

One day The Elder found Victory looking very sad beside the river. "Have you got troubles?" he asked.

"Yes. People keep taking my drawings."

The Elder moved slowly and carefully to sit beside Victory, honouring his space. They sat together quietly assessing the situation. It was the beginning of their connectedness. Victory suddenly felt he was in the presence of a like-minded spirit, and it warmed his heart.

Victory had been struggling within himself. He was fundamentally moral rather than political, and he had worked out that people were not stupid, just badly educated.

He saw realities. He was entranced by everything and found himself going through doors other people never saw and which automatically opened for him. It was a terrifying struggle to keep quiet about the things he knew and thought about.

He thought children's creativity was confined and so he set about doing his own in secret. But he could not hide his drawings, and everyone who saw them was astonished. He intuitively believed art to be a language capable of changing life, not merely recording it.

The Elder was a good judge of character, a good listener and so he saw Victory's self-control. Unlike many young people, Victory had goals, dreams and self-discipline. He had roots and aerials. He touched and knew the ground he came from, and he noticed breaks in the clouds and the stars in the heavens. The Elder was the first person to recognise the truth about Victory.

CHAPTER TEN

Victory's school teacher was established in teaching and had been well educated. He was a kind, caring man with firm and gentle ways. He had learned not to judge a book by its cover and to take baby steps when dealing with different or special children.

Even so, Victory was a complete mystery to him. At first he thought Victory was an actor or a pretender, because Victory seemed to be half there and half in another place. And Victory was not communicating. Yet, as he observed Victory in silence, he perceived something unusual about this boy.

Victory had a vast general knowledge. Victory had a great understanding of human nature. Victory had a remarkable ability in arts, language and maths, but only spoke when spoken to and answered in the simple language of the other children.

While the teacher was fascinated with Victory, he had a difficult class of children who had behaviour problems that were a real trial. Victory was well-behaved. Others had bad language, shouted out insults, did not trust, had no boundaries and were very disruptive.

Children in his class were frequently acting like victims of society. The teacher could see why, because society no longer put children at the centre of its visions or policies.

Apart from the Children's Art House and the skate park, there was little provision for children's activities and events in the town. There was an adult's Art Society run by retired people, where children were told to be quiet and not touch when they came to view the work. Parents had little time for their children when the orchards were humming with fruit picking.

A child can easily fall over without encouragement, and good sleep and good food was often lacking as well. But it was the aimlessness and the boredom which concerned the teacher about his pupils. They roamed around the neighbourhood in an idle fashion, unsupervised and looked for mischief.

Children in his class were resistant to schooling for no single reason. Whereas another teacher might have been tempted into blaming a single cause, he knew to be wary of oversimplifying situations. Nevertheless the teacher felt the huge burden of responsibility to change what he could for his pupils. Victory gave him no grief and, as he seemed to cope, the teacher decided to let him be.

Victory knew the teacher had decided to leave him to his own devices and just got on with observing everything in silence. Victory knew who the bullies were and the harm they were capable of inflicting. He also knew one day he would have to confront them, and how he might be hurt.

That day came. The gang got him as he rounded the corner of his street on his way home from school. They mobbed him and turned him upside down and shook him hard, and then they gave him a piece of white chalk and demanded he draw a picture for them on the footpath. He could hardly move his arms, let alone see, and he realised that the situation was potentially very dangerous for him. Quickly they ripped the backpack off him and passed his sketchbook around. They threw Little Fella into the ditch. The pain of that pierced him deeply; he could bear the pain in his ankles. He valiantly tried to draw to their demands.

Victory did not panic. He had prepared himself for this moment. He remained silent. Instinctively he knew about being ultra-positive while you are in a hell-hole.

Some of the boys were becoming very uncomfortable about what was happening, but Google was without any sensitivity and positively dangerous once he got a victim. They all feared Google.

Victory drew as demanded, a fish and a horse. The boys passed his sketchbook around. "Holy cow!" one said. They were becoming quiet, and more interested in the book than in Victory hanging upside down, drawing. The drawings on the footpath were better than any of them could ever do. Victory wondered what they were going to do next. Even while hanging upside down he kept his senses and knew things were falling apart for them.

It was Legend who saved him. Legend was training with the big boys in the field just across from the corner. He spotted the gang was closed in around someone and then glimpsed Victory hanging upside down in the middle of the circle. That was it for Legend. He shouted, "Leave him alone!" and began sprinting towards the fence of the field. Then the coach saw what was happening and yelled out, "Stop that!"

The gang dispersed quickly, dumping Victory hard on to the concrete. Legend got to him first. Victory sat quietly without complaint. Legend picked up the sketchbook and found Little Fella and the backpack.

Legend was furious. The coach talked to him. "It's not fair, and it's not right!" Legend said. Coach told him to go and punch ten holes hard into the air. "When you get this angry," he said, "do not hurt another person or break anything. Always punch air holes as hard as you can and get that anger out." Legend never forgot this lesson.

Both boys grew up that day when the world had caught up with them. Their childhood innocence had been violated.

After this event, Google left Victory alone, and so did the other children. One or two said, "Sorry mate", when they next passed Victory on the street.

Victory realised that his creativity had saved him and that Legend was a true friend for life. But Victory also knew the real nature of Google. For Google, totally unstructured vandalism was a fun activity when he was bored. And he also understood that Google could not afford to lose face and so would retaliate one day.

Victory chose not to tell his parents about the incident. Dad was away in the back hills and Mum was asleep when he got home. She had coughed all through the previous night.

He made himself a meal in the way she had trained him to. He left the kitchen tidy and went to his room where he talked with Little Fella and Parrie. His ankles were red and sore and he had a graze or two. He put lavender oil on them, washed himself well and then went to his bed and drew.

Victory's mind wandered up to space and he looked down on humanity from afar. He felt that the taming of mankind would bring about peace on earth. He realised that the planet was endangered until such time as mankind could be kind to each other. He wrote a new code for humanity in his mind that night. It started with respect and tolerance for all cultures, the appreciation of human differences, and the honouring of the earth first. He thought that gardeners were the most important people, and that artists and thinkers should be considered our visionaries. He saw children in advance of society, and as such they should be consulted and included in any policy making.

He had always thought war futile, and now he began analysing the root causes of war and found that lack of love was at the centre. Google had no love in his life. Did that make Google evil? He wondered what he could do to make Google nicer. Be friends? Give him a drawing? He had never been unkind to Google or anyone, but Google had never been kind to anyone. Victory thought just one small act of kindness coming from Google would surprise everyone and might change Google.

Victory spent the night in thought. But before he could fall asleep, he checked on his sleeping mother and saw that she was breathing well and was warm.

A short time later Victory's sketchbook was stolen from his backpack. And Little Fella was gone. He told Legend when they were out riding the beach.

"Man, I will take their lights out," Legend said. He was furious and then for a short time he punched air holes as his coach had taught him.

"I am not angry, just sad. I feel like running away where no one can get my work. I will butter bread to get another sketchbook," Victory said quietly.

Whenever a hangi was coming, he had the job of buttering the bread. Mum had a birthday soon, and that would mean work for him. Victory knew his father wished to do more for his mother.

He also knew that his father was afraid of the changes out in the bush. The deforestation was causing slips, and the rivers were washing the soil out to sea. The rivers themselves were being contaminated with toxic materials. Sprays used for the orchards were leaching into the soil. Chemicals were poisoning rare native plants. Possums and rabbits had done damage since they were introduced years before by the early settlers. Birds were dying, and some species had become extinct. Introduced plants like gorse and privet had invaded vast areas and even the bees were on the decrease.

While his father did not talk to Victory about this, Victory overheard the men's conversations when they came to the back yard for a drink with Dad. No one asked Victory what he thought, except The Elder when they met down by the river.

Victory told The Elder that his sketchbook and his Little Fella had been taken. "You need to get a new book?" The Elder asked.

"Yes. I am buttering bread for the money. But I

will need a safe place to hide it."

"I know one. I can show you. I used to need it once," The Elder said quietly.

They sat together by the river in thought and then arranged to see the secret place. It was there in the bush that The Elder shared many stories with Victory. He told Victory that he knew he was beautiful because his grandmother had told him that when he was seven. She had told him he was precious, unique and important. She had told him that he was lucky to be alive because it was a privilege to live; that there was only one of him, ever and that he was magnificent. She also told him she loved him dearly, now and always. She told him that the most important food was a smile and a hug.

She taught him not to be in competition with others but to be cooperative and, where possible, to lend a helping hand. She taught him to stand up and say his bit quietly and then sit down and listen. She cautioned him to keep things simple and to play fair. She told him that humbleness was a virtue and pride was arrogant. She taught him to carry no fear.

She taught him the stories of her ancestors and of how, in the long term, those who plunder never win. She taught him to eat well, rest, exercise and live moderately. She cautioned him about carrying anger or a critical spirit because these always come back and land on you. Her favourite saying was "Look up, not down; look out, not in; look forward, not backwards, and lend a helping hand."

Victory listened in silence, and The Elder knew he collected every thought and would remember it. Victory told The Elder of his dreams, and The Elder showed him great respect. "You are not alone," he said. "No man is an island." He said that each man's joy is your joy; each man's grief is your grief. He spoke about how everyone was inextricably mixed. How we were all the same and the one "I Am".

These moments in time were ultimately precious to Victory. He had found his mentor. There was not a subject that Victory could not discuss with The Elder. The insights The Elder gave him came in stories he could remember. They were life stories, relevant to this place, and with visual imagery and mystical depth. This was the language Victory understood in his mind. He did not like the fixed, frozen, static camera images of today's society; rather, he loved images that had time, space, scale and myth to them. While he could think in minute detail, he was a quantum thinker and thought in the scale of total humanity which also honoured individuality. They spoke about conformity, about true freedom of thought, and about responsibility. The Elder taught him there was no such thing as a right without a responsibility, it was a privilege to lead and serve, and lack of self-control and self-discipline caused problems for the soul.

His encounters with The Elder always quieted Victory. He did not tell his parents that he sat and talked with him down by the river, and his parents never asked, for they were used to him going off with Legend to play.

One day, Victory and Legend went downtown to look at art gear for Victory. He had been saving his money, and after Mum's party he would have enough to buy a new sketchbook.

They walked past the large murals done by the children who went to the Children's Art House. There were many murals in the town since the

Children's Art House opened and the town looked more colourful, and this made people feel happy.

Seeing the town being a canvas for creativity was a turning point in Victory's childhood. He was not surprised that the children's art was so good. He knew that children brought the fresh and new into existence and that they had wonderful ideas and abilities when given a chance to show or present them. Some of the children at his school loved art as their most favourite subject, and were very happy when doing it. The graffiti in the town had dropped because the children had a connection to the town now, and things looked as if they were improving for everyone.

Victory and Legend went into the Curiosity Shop. They knew everything there was cheaper, and they did not have much money. They enjoyed searching the shelves and stroking the books and finding some pens and a book that would be just right. They did not see The Elder shopping in the back corner.

But the owners had been hit hard by Google and his team's shoplifting and were nervous about the young boys looking around. They shooed them out of the shop.

The boys were upset. It hurt to be treated as bad people when neither of them had a bad bone in their bodies. They did not know that The Elder had seen all and then moved to find the book and pens which they had been coveting, and he went to the counter and bought them.

The Elder lived on a benefit and used up his entire month's spending money to purchase these things. He counted out the coins carefully on the counter and asked the shop assistant to wrap the goods very well.

Then, with a gentlemanly, "Good day" to her, he tipped his hat and left. He would take the articles to the secret hiding place and give them to Victory one day soon.

Victory was glad the weather was fine for Mum's hangi. She deserved a party. She was over her chest infection and had been looking forward to this day.

But her day was spoilt by the school teacher, reporting to Matua that Victory was always dreaming and not concentrating on school work. Yes, since the upturning Victory had found it hard to sit in the classroom with the boys who had been so unkind to him, and he often tuned out when they started playing up in the lessons. It was beginning to seem a waste of time going to school at all. But today was Mum's day, and he was going to butter all the bread and get his money. Mum went out to get the watercress, a job she loved.

Dad and Victory were alone preparing for the hangi before the visitors arrived. Victory sat with a pile of bread in front of him and started buttering when Dad came over. "Son," Dad said in a voice that was ominous, "listen up. I hear you are dreaming again in school. Why don't you concentrate on your school work? You are always thinking about your art. Where is your art going to get you? How are you going to make money from your art? Do you think you could feed a family on your art?"

Victory kept his head down and kept buttering.

"How much does a slice of bread cost? How many slices in a lunch sandwich? How many slices in a loaf of bread? How much money do you need to make each week to survive? How much money does it take to feed a family?"

Dad picked up a slice and waved it around in Victory's face. Victory was given no time to answer Dad's questions. He shrugged, sighed and kept buttering.

Just then the visitors started to arrive, and he felt saved. They did not notice him sitting there, buttering away. The men brought in boxes of beer. Dad will get drunk again, Victory thought, and Mum deserves a party without problems. His Dad's voice kept ringing in his ears.

Victory knew Dad cared about him and was worried about him, but he loathed these scenes and felt crushed by them. Most of all he was disappointed that his father was disappointed in him. He longed for his father's approval.

Scenes like this just drove him into deeper silences. He knew Dad worked hard to keep his mother and him. He heard that Dad was the hardest worker the forestry company had, and he believed that. He wished he could help his dad, but he was only a primary school boy. Dad would not hit him, but emotionally he felt depleted after scenes like these.

His father did not know Victory, because Victory could not communicate with his father and tell him all the amazing things he had in his head. Dad had a preconceived idea of what Victory should be like to be a man. Victory thought of his Dad growing up in his mountain valley with his father. Dad was just like his father everyone kept saying. Not a bad man, a real bush man, not an arty-farty type. To be one of those was to be a wimp in Victory's father's eyes. Yet it was Victory's grandfather who had encouraged The Elder.

The visitors brought in a great assortment of food. It was a custom around here to feast with plenty when there was a celebration. Trays of shellfish, kina, mussels and crayfish arrived. The crayfish was already boiled and had turned that wonderful orange-red colour. Their beautiful textured shells fascinated Victory.

Dad took the pig off the ute. Beside it were trays of kumara, the beautiful purple kind of kumara, the colour Victory adored. Trays of cabbage and kiwi fruit came in. Pumpkins, which were already cut up, arrived and the men began digging and heating up the stones.

The children from The Elder's house came and hung balloons on the fence. The guitars came out and people started singing. The singing was the best part, along with the food.

But the food took a long time to cook under the ground and soon the drinking took over. Dad's friends were the hard back-country men of the district. They enjoyed getting together once or twice a year to party up.

When Mum came home with the cress, everyone hugged her and kissed her. She was pleased to see her husband so happy. She did not notice how withdrawn Victory was. Victory could hear The Elder's words: "Rise above it."

He braced himself. He knew that tonight, drunk, snoring people would sleep in his room. In the morning there would be a huge mess to clean up. He would not be able to sleep for the noise and some people would stay on a day or two. These people were not bad people, just caught up in a culture that encouraged them to party hard.

They were a hazardous mess, reckless and silly to behave like this, Victory thought. But he continued to do his duties of picking up cans and getting plates and passing around food. A hangi is a big piece of work, he thought, and it is good that everyone shares the cost of food and drink. The thought that next week he would be able to buy those pens and a sketchbook kept Victory going.

The party left casualties in relationships and Mum and Dad too tired to talk after the visitors finally left. Victory got his room back to himself. He was tired and dreaming wildly if he did sleep at all.

CHAPTER ELEVEN

At school the teacher spoke to him. "You must stop all this day dreaming and focus on your work, this is what your father and mother want." The teacher said this in front of the class and it hurt Victory. All Victory lived for now was his meetings in the bush with The Elder.

After the hangi, The Elder asked him to meet him at their hideaway, where Victory went with heavy heart because the book and pens had been bought by someone else. He dragged along to the spot. He was at war with his mind.

There was The Elder with a parcel! Victory was delighted.

"Keep your money, you must save as much as you can," The Elder told Victory. He sat and watched as Victory began drawing. "Would you like to draw too?" Victory asked, and they decided to draw each other.

While they worked they talked about portraits and images, about the power of communication without words, and of the responsibility of an artist, and how artists are often underpaid, unsung heroes. He taught Victory to expect the unexpected. All this stimulated Victory's mind and he had many questions. "Art is long, sport is short," The Elder told him. "Art is life," he added.

The Elder decided to tell Victory what had happened to him in life during his time working in the arts. Parts of his story were exciting, because for some incredible years he was commissioned to work representing his country on large-scale collaborative pieces for embassies and corporations.

He told of practical obstacles, of events, of resources running out and of lack of integrity of sponsors and staff. He told of community-based experiences and of how people's dreams and talents had succeeded or failed, depending on the planning, the standards set and maintained, and on their behaviours. He spoke of how some of his early work had been stolen, including his own childhood sketchbook.

After several visits they finished their portraits and gave them to each other. They laughed, encouraged each other and praised each other's efforts. "It is important to be human first and professional second," The Elder told him as they finished their portraits.

Victory wondered about The Elder's sayings and how he always managed to tell stories which fitted occasions. It is wisdom born from experience, he surmised.

He wished he could take all The Elder's knowledge and make it his own. He thought it was sad that we repeat so many mistakes because we do not learn from each other, and that we all had to go through things over and over again as a species. Why couldn't we find a way of collecting up our combined experience to move us forward?

He wished he could record every small nuance on The Elder's face, or pickle it so that he could keep it. But how do you keep a smile or a laugh or capture the wrinkles around smiling eyes? He loved the way those old brown eyes twinkled with glee or welled up with tears of sadness. He loved the veins in the old man's hands, which were like a travel map. He loved the voice which spoke gently and had no force but which delivered such wonderful words.

Most of all, Victory loved the positivity of the old man who took the time to notice him and walk and talk with him. In this man there was no complaint, criticism, blame, pain, shame or put-down. No fear, doubt, uncertainty. No guilt, no anger. There was only simple human kindness. There was love as Victory had never seen it expressed anywhere else.

His mother loved him. Victory knew she loved him truly, as best she could. But she did not have the capacity to love the whole of humanity the way this man did. It was as if Victory was looking into his soul, into himself, as he spoke with The Elder, and he found it altogether wondrous, their magical friendship.

During these times Victory no longer felt at war with his mind. They had talked about loneliness of mind as being the cruellest place in the world. "The world is not waiting for us, we must create our own future," the old man said as they left their special sitting log.

He told Victory he would be away for some time

as he had to go visit a relative. That night The Elder
and his wife walked the river bank very slowly and
heard the moreporks crying. They held hands and
helped each other along.

CHAPTER TWELVE

The Elder walked across the field the next day to the Children's Art House. There were many Children's Art Houses dotted throughout the country now. He had started the first one and others followed after people had seen how children loved them.

Today was a special meeting in the local Children's Art House, because finances were low. On the big table, where usually ten children sat working on their individual art pieces, was a pile of papers. The committee members had arrived and were talking.

"We have got to raise some funds quickly."

"People are not paying fees."

"We need more materials."

"We cannot get others to help."

"The government should do something."

The Elder stood up and leaned against the wall for support, then spoke quietly. "It is not about putea; it is about aroha. It is not about money; it is about love. It is not about paper; it is about people. It is not about us; it is about children. It is not about talking; it is about doing." He took a rolled up paper out of his pocket. They watched him reel it out and pin it on the notice board above the bookcase. THE DEPARTMENT OF DOING. "It is not about talking; it is about doing."

He sat down in silence. Everyone was quiet for a while. The committee changed the topic. "What should we do about Victory? He does not always pay fees. He is too quiet."

"He is a very good artist. But people take his work, so he has got nothing to show for himself. He is a strange lad. He needs help. The teacher does not know how to help him."

The Elder quietly said, "I see God through him." Everyone looked at the old man. They revered him for his wisdom, and a comment like this made them stop and think. The Children's Art House had the Culture of Peace as its vision. No one talked about God here.

The Elder closed the meeting with a blessing and left. The longest serving member was an older woman. "Would anybody like a cup of tea?" she asked, and she rose to put the jug on. She had served up more cups of tea than anyone else in the district.

CHAPTER THIRTEEN

Victory continued going to the bush and working on,
alone. Sometimes he would be there for hours and
not realise the time. Only Legend knew where he was.
Victory began to miss the old man and was hoping he
would return soon because he was doing his best
work ever to show him.

One day Legend came to sit with him. Legend was
very uncomfortable. Distressed. Victory sensed it
immediately.

Legend took a deep breath. "I am sorry to tell you
this matey," he said. "He won't be coming back. He
died last night. I heard my mother and our neighbour
talking about it this morning."

Victory clasped his hands tight and closed his eyes.
He took a long deep breath. Legend put his hand on
Victory's knee. "I am truly sorry Victory. He loved
you more than the rest of us. He believed in you."

Victory started stroking his hands.

Legend sat beside him shuffling his feet, his teeth
clenched.

He had no words. There were no words.

They sat for a while, as still as statues.

"Mate, I have to go. Coach is waiting. Victory, the sky will not fall down. It's only air." Legend patted his friend's knee and went off quietly. He knew he could not help his friend. He thought, "I'll come back after training if I can."

But he did not get back that day.

Victory had tears of anguish in his heart, mind and soul. He felt fearful and frantic. His heart raced.

He broke his pencil in half and tossed it into the bush. He stood up, took his stick and began scratching a pattern in the dirt but he had no strength and felt faint. He became unstable on his feet.

He knew this was grief and his special bond was now broken. He knew he had to be gentle with himself. He felt his colour leave him and he lay down and slowly poured leaves over himself and buried himself in them. He kept his eyes closed.

He heard The Elder's voice saying, "You will find that the loneliest place on earth is the war in your mind."

Victory floated away and joined the clouds as they passed silently overhead. He was safe there.

Losing the one person who had faith in his ability and his potential, the one person who truly understood him, left Victory depleted. He began walking the beach, the bush and the river bed, alone. Victory cut a pathetic figure with hands behind his back and head down.

He seldom spoke and he stopped drawing. His sketchbook grew dusty and became covered with leaves in the hiding place. He did not go back to that place of sorrow.

Legend was busy training now and was happy to be selected for the top squad. The bullies left Victory alone. Google thought he had defeated Victory and that it was not worth troubling him anymore.

All the children knew Victory had stopped drawing. He did not go to the Art House anymore either. He did not play with Parrie.

The teacher sent home a school report of great concern. Victory's mother and father sat on the back porch and discussed it when he was asleep. Victory had been tossing and turning in bed under the blankets and was having nightmares again. In these dreams, he could hear his father's voice riding over everything. "How are you going to make money out of art?" It tormented him.

His mother listened to her mate's anxious cries about his son. "He needs help," she said, "and I am going to get it for him."

"He is not dumb," Matua said. "Why can't he snap out of himself?"

They did not know about the effect The Elder's death had on Victory, because they had no idea of how close he had become to the old man. "Perhaps I should take him back into the bush and toughen him up with the men," his dad said.

"What good would that do at the moment? He is not strong enough to cope with their ways."

They agreed there was more to Victory than they could understand, and that parenting was not easy. Both agreed he was a good son, obedient and loyal, and that he had good manners.

"He is still waters running deep," his father said. "Those waters are dangerous."

His mother advocated for him. "I don't know

what to do to help him, but I believe his creativity will
save him."

CHAPTER FOURTEEN

Victory was referred to a psychologist, a man of considerable experience, who was employed by the Education Department to look at mental health issues of the youth. This senior man spent half the year in his home on the beach about 100 miles away and the rest in England. He had studied the human condition for nearly 50 years and was vitally interested in the people of the land. Tangata whenua. In some ways, they gave him hope as he watched the human race drifting into a crisis. He saw the lack of balance between the creative mind and a healthy body as a gap that needed to be closed, and he thought that more should be done to assist children. Most of the children he worked with had labels. He saw all cases. He saw eating syndromes and disorders of every kind. Bipolar and suicidal tendencies, attention deficit disorder and lack of focus were common these days. Most children came to him already with a label given to them from schools or family. In this area, they were frequently beautiful looking children, usually physically well built, and they could sing.

His wife was engaged in the mental health arena too. For many years, they took an evening promenade before bed. They exchanged various cases they had seen, and this always helped them both. It is good to be on the same page, they thought. They never discussed cases with anyone else because they were grounded in professionalism.

The psychologist had learnt to ask questions and listen to the undermind of children. Today, he was meeting a boy who had become non-verbal. It was unusual to get a referral from this remote place. The notes were sketchy. "Boy, aged nine, slight, non-verbal, a loner."

He was fascinated but knew not to assume anything. Children generally do not shut themselves off in the way that this boy was described, not without good reason. "Sadly," he thought as he drove to the address, "it's usually because of fear and abuse."

He turned up his music and concentrated on the beautiful scenery. He knew not to go into the negative.

He thought about the conference he had just attended in Portugal, representing his country. He was asked if it was a country at war because of the figures and facts on child abuse, neglect and violence. He wondered what good his years of work had been if the country was sinking into such ways. It was seldom he saw a normal child. That was not his job.

He was a creative man. He loved music, arts, gardening and making things. He always took his camera with him and entered and won many competitions. He should have retired a few years ago but the government could not find a suitable replacement; no one applied to go into this area of the country.

"Are you Victory?" he asked.

"Sure," Victory nodded. Victory was not completely sure why he was there. He had a clue that it was because everyone was concerned about him, especially his parents.

"I'm Mr Fraser. May I ask you some questions?"

The seasoned psychologist leaned in towards Victory once he was comfortably seated beside him. Victory instantly remembered The Elder telling him always to tell the truth if ever he felt cornered, and always to use manners. "Never be repugnant," The Elder had said.

"Yes sir."

The psychologist noticed Victory's politeness and willingness to cooperate. "Tell me, Victory, what do you do when you are alone?"

Victory assessed him and wondered what the man was seeking. Best to tell the truth, he thought. "I go up and down," Victory said, with his eyes looking upwards.

"What do you mean? How do you go up and down?" The psychologist pencilled B/P on his notepad. "Where do you start, up or down?"

"I usually start on the ground," said Victory. "First, I look at the stones, the soil, the clay, the dirt, the rocks, and I notice the tiny insects, the patterns, the shapes, and the colours of the place where they live. I see their stabbers or suckers and the way they live together. I look at their homes. Some of them are very well constructed." Victory had found his voice.

He started speaking to the psychologist just as he

had spoken to The Elder, because Mr Fraser just sat there and listened. He heard Victory's amazing descriptions of the minute plants, ferns, bushes, seeds and stems. He could vividly imagine the colours of each one. Mr Fraser was transported to another world as Victory fluently described the trees, the birds, the canopy, and the clouds and then began on the universe he saw. Then Victory said, "I start to come down again because it has all changed. Everything is fleeting and transient. It can take me all day, if I am not interrupted."

Mr Fraser did not write anything. After a few minutes of silence, he asked, "Victory, who do you talk to?"

"I used to talk to Little Fella but now he is gone."

"Was he real?" Mr Fraser asked.

"No, I invented him."

"Victory, do you talk to the man upstairs?"

Victory wondered what kind of question that was, but answered. "No sir. My family are poor; we do not have an upstairs."

In all his research Mr Fraser had heard about children like Victory, but he had not met one before. Mr Fraser saw clearly that Victory had a global view and a deep consciousness. Their time went well over schedule and there were other clients to see.

"You may go now."

"Thank you sir. But can I ask you a question?"

"Of course you can."

"Why do you wear those glasses?"

After an interesting conversation about eyesight Victory left and Mr Fraser sat to write up his report. Curious, fascinated with life, advanced language, inquiring mind. Possibly gifted. No treatment necessary.

Mr Fraser snapped his brief case closed and drove home. He cancelled his other clients and that night as he walked the beach with his wife, he told her, "I think I need to retire. I am so used to seeing dysfunctional children that when I meet a normal child I think it is rare.

"Today, I met a very gifted child and it shocked me that this boy had grown up with no support, and without detection. This boy has huge potential and is a visionary with a deep consciousness. I was careful about what I wrote because I did not want to burden him with a label."

"I am glad you met him," said his wife. "That's a lovely finish to your career."

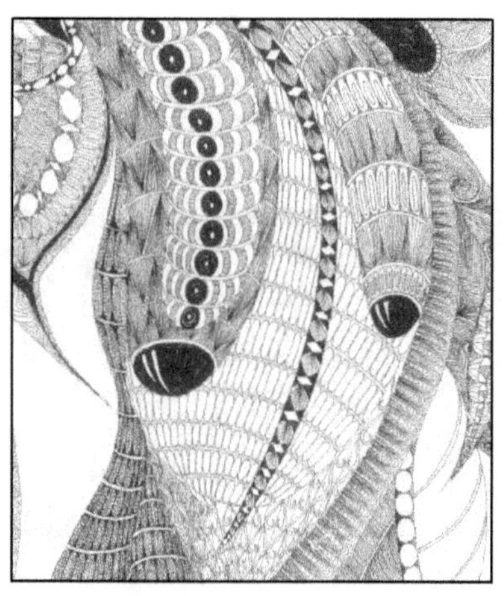

CHAPTER FIFTEEN

That night Victory went to his room early and tossed and turned under the blankets. That was a nice man, he thought, but had he said too much? His father's words rang in his ears, and he wished he could erase them: "How can you make money out of art?"

He wondered where Little Fella was and pictured him in a ditch, broken and growing mould.

There was a knock at the door. Victory peeped out and saw the old woman. She was talking to Dad. "Are you Matua, Victory's father?" she asked.

"Yes, Miss, I am. I am sorry about your loss," Matua replied.

"Yes," she said, "The moreporks cried. He left peacefully."

She held a parcel. "This was returned to our family recently. It was stolen from my husband when he was a boy. He wanted to give it to Victory. We have had a family meeting, and we would like Victory to have it. My family believes Dad would be happy to have us give it to him now because he thought the world of your boy."

Matua was genuinely surprised. He did not know that Victory even knew the old man. But he said, "Thank you, Thank you very much." He kissed the old lady and watched her go slowly off down the road.

Matua brought the parcel into Victory. "This is a parcel for you. It's a gift from The Elder`s family."

"Thank you, Dad."

"How well did you know that man?" Matua asked his son.

"Very," Victory said. His father left the room. In his bed, Victory carefully untied the string around the brown paper. Inside was The Elder's first sketchbook. Victory turned the pages very slowly and stroked each drawing. He knew some of the places and faces The Elder had sketched. He read the comments written alongside some drawings. He felt the pain of the statements which said, "No one is helping me. I am giving up." He turned the old pages over very preciously.

At the end of the book, he found new comments. "Art is long. Sport is short." Then he found tucked inside the cover the portrait that he had done of his friend. And for the first time he cried.

The next day Victory got up early and ran across the field, along the river bank and to the grave. It was a single grave in a paddock beside the river. The Elder had loved that river and his days of whitebaiting, eeling, swimming, riding and walking here. The family had decided not to bury him up in the hills where they could seldom visit him. This was a peaceful spot here by the river. There were flax flowers placed beautifully on top of the grave and a white cross.

Victory took out a small piece of paper from his pocket and placed it on the grave. It said simply, "Thank you."

He turned and went to the bush, to their hiding place and dragged out his sketchbook. It had laid there covered in leaves untouched for some months. He dusted it down. Then he sat and began sketching again as fresh ideas poured out onto his pages.

He kept his hiding place a secret from all but Legend.

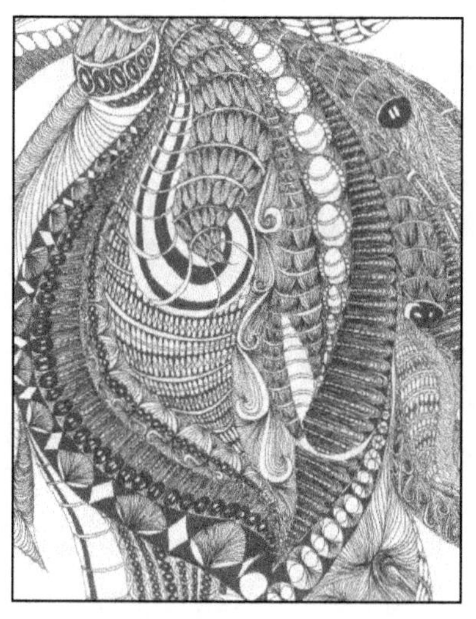

CHAPTER SIXTEEN

Time passed quickly, as it always does. Victory and Legend began cleaning windows to make money. Victory started working each Saturday morning. One fresh morning, Victory, who always had a marvellous drawing hanging out of his pocket, was cleaning a window. As he cleaned, he looked inside and saw an artist working. The artist had dreadlocks; he was a sensitive portrait artist. His studio was filled with wondrous works. The artist saw Victory peeping in and waved back with a big smile. They both smiled and waved to each other. From the kitchen, the artist's mother called to her son, "Victory, cup of tea time." When Victory looked back to see the boy he was no longer there; he had gone. Amongst the treasures in that room on the studio table were the portraits that Victory and The Elder had exchanged. On the shelf, along with piles of books, was The Elder's sketchbook. Parrie was tucked into the corner. Outside was a sports car with "Legend's Gym" painted on its doors.

EPILOGUE

During the days that brought Victory to this time, he had studied, received a first-class PhD and became known as "The Star of the East". He became the Father of a renaissance of indigenous art. He did not marry. Legend married Maria, played for the All Blacks and had two beautiful children. It was a good marriage and Victory looked out for them. Legend's son was called Vic-iti. Victory was admired as a quietly spoken gentleman who worked long hours for the environment and education using his phenomenal creative ability. He was often likened to Rua, the prophet, one of his forefathers. He was without religion. He was himself: spiritually enlightened. Victory worked to rebuild Hiona the village up in the Ureweras as a living monument, just as he had discussed with The Elder. Matua and his bush men friends supported Victory`s work because the big trees were scarce, and the wood should be put to good community use.

Magnificently crafted whares appeared up in the wahi tapu community of Maungapohatu. Only once during this time there was a conflict, which concerned local gangs and trespassing. It was a momentous occasion when blood could have been shed. The tension was finally broken by a big man on his mountain horse. His name was Google. Until that day Google had been silent. Over the years Victory noticed that Google had never spoken to him. He also knew that Google had formed a gang, had been in trouble and went bush. But as it turned out, it was Google who saved the project. "Do not prevent this man's work," he insisted. "He is the best man around here." Everyone laid down their complaints. "Do what he asks," Google directed his men and saluted Victory. And that was that.

Victory built a significant local Children's Art House and its fame spread across the world. He supported the National Showcase for Maori Arts and Crafts Education. He organised bronze sculptures for large galleries of the world. His self-portrait sculpture was sent to the United Nations Building in New York.

Victory was slight in build and had a hole in his heart. He died of a heart infection at 36 years old.

"Only the good die young," Legend said to Vic-iti.

"I'll probably live a long time, but I will never forget him," Google said at Victory's tangi.

Victory was laid to rest in the grove where his brothers and sisters had grown tall while waiting.

GLOSSARY

Most New Zealanders will be familiar with the terms used in this book. However, interest in this is international, so we have included a glossary to assist our readers in other countries. Sources for more and better explanations can be found at
Māori Dictionary Online
http://www.maoridictionary.co.nz/

Te whanake – Māori language online
http://www.tewhanake.maori.nz/

Aroha - love
Hāngī- earthen oven feast
Hiona- Zion
Iti waewae- little leg
Kete - woven flax basket
Kowhaiwhai -repeating pattern
Kumara - native sweet potato
Mana - prestige
Marae -courtyard in front of meeting house
Mokopuna - grandchildren
Morepork - native owl
Pākehā - foreigner, non-māori
Putea – fund
Rimu - native tree
Tangi - funeral
Totara - native tree
Tangata Whenua - people of the land
Ureweras – historic home of Tuhoe
Whānau - extended family
Ute - pick-up truck, utility vehicle

ABOUT THE AUTHOR

Shona Hammond Boys, QSM (New Zealand), PVSA (USA), is a distinguished teacher, artist, and the National Director and Founder of the New Zealand Children's Art House Foundation.

She has travelled worldwide lecturing and presenting the Children's Art House concept. Her dream to see Children's Art Houses in each community of New Zealand has flourished.

With 50 years of service of experience working with community arts and culture, Shona has a deep concern for talented children who grow up in isolation. *Oku Moe Moea, "The dream which is bigger than I Am"* is set in Opotiki, which is one of New Zealand`s lowest socio-economic areas, and addresses her concerns.

Shona is passionate about art as the foundation tool for education, peace, the environment, for all people. She endorses the theme of the International Child Art Foundation: *A Creative Mind in a Healthy Body.*

Funds from this book support
Children's Art Houses
www.arthouses.org.nz
www.icaf.org

NOTES

MORE BMS BOOKS

Enjoyed this book? The following list of books is available from BMS Books.

Always a Grunt by Mike Ledingham

Once a Grunt by Mike Ledingham

A Soldier's Life by Lou Geraets

My Life…the Meanderings of Pop Knill by Lou Geraets

The Last Newspaper in the World by Mick Stone

Autumn and Other Stories by Rotorua Writers Group

The Forgotten by Sarah Groot

Demons Inside My Mind – Life with Anorexia – Jenna Oldham

LOCAL BOOKS

Local Books is a service provided by BMS to help self-published writers and other independent publishers to market their books. For more information about BMS Books and Local Books, contact:

BMS Books
5 High Street, Glenholme
Rotorua 3010
New Zealand
Email: ms@bms.co.nz and URL: www.bms.co.nz
Tel: 64-7-349 4107